Look at that toothy, terrifying creature! Is it a dragon?

DRAGON?!
Where?

Tarbosaurus
(tar-bow-SORE-us)

3

No, it's a dinosaur!
Unlike dragons, dinosaurs
were real. But fear not:
Their kind has been gone
for a long, long time.

Hey, no SPOILERS!

Tyrannosaurus rex
(tye-RAN-oh-SORE-us)

Although they no longer roam Earth, these fantastic beasts still capture our imaginations!

Some were as big as a building!

Some had ginormous jaws!

Some were covered in armor and spikes!

Let's face it:

Dinosaurs are...

SO COOL!

8

AWWW, SHUCKS.

Nurosaurus
(NEW-row-SORE-us)

9

Dinosaurs were reptiles that ruled the world millions of years ago. The word "dinosaur" means "terrible lizard."

Agujaceratops
(ah-GOO-ja-SER-ah-tops)

Spinosaurus
(SPINE-oh-SORE-us)

Megalosaurus
(MEG-ah-low-SORE-us)

AGE OF THE DINOSAURS

The first dinosaurs appeared around 240 million years ago, when all Earth's land was squished into one giant mass surrounded by ocean. Dinosaurs reigned for more than 160 million years, much longer than humans have been around.

Who are you calling TERRIBLE?

Chilesaurus
(CHILL-ay-SORE-us)

Dinosaurs came in all shapes and sizes, and not all of them were big. Many, like the nimble *Compsognathus*, weren't much larger than a chicken.

What's a
CHICKEN?

Compsognathus
(KOMP-sog-NAH-thus)

13

Some dinosaurs ate other dinosaurs. They had razor-sharp teeth and ran on two legs.

TOOTHY TERROR

Tyrannosaurus rex, the most famous of the meat-munching dinosaurs, was as long as a school bus from head to tail and as tall as a two-story building. It could spring after other dinosaurs at 25 miles an hour (40 km/h) and clamp down on prey with massive, bone-crunching teeth—which were the size of bananas!

Nice to EAT you!

Dracoraptor
(DRAH-ko-RAP-tor)

15

But that doesn't mean you'd have to run from every dinosaur you met. In fact, most ate only plants. They had special teeth for grinding up leaves.

Stegosaurus
(STEG-oh-SORE-us)

Brachiosaurus
(BRACK-ee-oh-SORE-us)

Parasaurolophus
(PAR-ah-saw-RAH-loh-fuss)

In this dino-eat-dino world, many dinosaurs had bodies covered in armor and spikes for protection. *Ankylosaurus* wielded its heavy tail like a club!

Ankylosaurus
(AN-kye-loh-SORE-us)

Dinosaurs hatched from eggs like most reptiles. Some dinosaurs even sat on their eggs until they hatched—like scary chickens.

They grow up SO FAST.

Maiasaura
(MA-ya-SORE-a)

Dinosaurs didn't look
the way they often do
in movies. Scientists
think many had feathers!

Anchiornis
(ANN-kee-OR-niss)

Pterosaur
(TARE-oh-sore)

Not every big reptile that lived during the time of the dinosaurs was a dinosaur.

24

MISTAKEN IDENTITY

There were other reptiles that lived during the age of the dinosaurs. While these three are from the same family tree that includes the dinosaurs, they're not considered dinosaurs.

CROCODILES: These fearsome reptiles of today lived during the age of the dinosaurs—and even hunted them!

PTEROSAURS: With wingspans that could reach nearly 40 feet (12 m), these incredible creatures were the biggest animal to ever fly the sky!

PLESIOSAURS: From nose to tail, these long-necked sea creatures could be as long as 50 feet (15 m) and may have had the strongest bite force of any animal that ever lived.

Dinosaurs disappeared 66 million years ago after a city-size asteroid crashed into Earth.

Dinosaurs are long gone, but they left behind lots of evidence for scientists to study: fossilized bones, dino-bits preserved in tree sap, and even dino poop!

DIGGING FOR DINO EVIDENCE!

Here are some of the ways scientists learn about dinosaurs.

STONE BONES: When dinos died, their bodies slowly turned mostly to stone—or petrified—over time and were preserved forever.

If these old **BONES** could talk.

Stegosaurus bones

Stegosaurus

Stegosaurus had a narrow body and a heavy, spiked tail. Its back legs were almost twice as long as its front legs. The plates down its back stood on its hind legs to reach tall vegetation.

Stegosaurus stenops

SAP TRAPS: Tree sap drips down and hardens, preserving everything trapped within it. This tough substance is called amber.

DINO DOO-DOO: Scientists love finding fossilized poo, called coprolite. Each nugget reveals a bit more about a dinosaur's diet.

Not all dinosaurs died out. You can see some outside your window today. Believe it or not, today's birds are modern dinosaurs.

Hummingbird

Parakeet

Penguin

DINO DESCENDANTS

Every bird you see today is a dinosaur. Seriously! The earliest birds first appeared around 150 million years ago as small, feathered, winged dinosaurs. They survived the asteroid that wiped out their bigger siblings 66 million years ago.

Deinocheirus
(DINE-oh-KYE-russ)

NATIONAL GEOGRAPHIC and Yellow Border Design are trademarks of the National Geographic Society, used under license.

Since 1888, the National Geographic Society has funded more than 14,000 research, conservation, education, and storytelling projects around the world. National Geographic Partners distributes a portion of the funds it receives from your purchase to National Geographic Society to support programs including the conservation of animals and their habitats. To learn more, visit natgeo.com/info.

For more information, visit nationalgeographic.com, call 1-877-873-6846, or write to the following address:

National Geographic Partners, LLC
1145 17th Street N.W.
Washington, D.C. 20036-4688 U.S.A.

For librarians and teachers: nationalgeographic.com/books/librarians-and-books

More for kids from National Geographic: natgeokids.com

National Geographic Kids magazine inspires children to explore their world with fun yet educational articles on animals, science, nature, and more. Using fresh storytelling and amazing photography, *Nat Geo Kids* shows kids ages 6 to 14 the fascinating truth about the world—and why they should care. **natgeo.com/subscribe**

For rights or permissions inquiries, please contact National Geographic Books Subsidiary Rights: bookrights@natgeo.com

Written by Crispin Boyer
Designed by Julide Dengel

The publisher would like to thank everyone who worked to make this book come together: Ariane Szu-Tu, editor; Shannon Hibberd, photo editor; Molly Reid, production editor; Anne LeongSon and Gus Tello, design production assistants; Shannon Pallatta, design assistant; and a special thank you to Nizar Ibrahim PhD, vertebrate paleontologist, National Geographic Explorer, Assistant Professor of Biology (University of Detroit Mercy), and Visiting Researcher (University of Portsmouth).

Cover (UP LE), Catmando/Shutterstock; (UP RT), YuRi Photolife/Shutterstock; (LO LE), 3Dalia/Shutterstock; (LO RT), SCIEPRO/Getty Images; (sunglasses), Kaissa/Shutterstock; (bow tie), LHF Graphics/Shutterstock; spine, DM7/Shutterstock; back cover (LE), LindaMarieB/Getty Images; (RT), Michael Rosskothen/Shutterstock; (hat), Les Perysty/Shutterstock; footprints (throughout), klerik78/Shutterstock; folios (throughout), IrynMerry/Shutterstock; 1, DM7/Shutterstock; 3, Michael Rosskothen/Adobe Stock; 4 (UP), Tribalium88/Shutterstock; 5, warpaintcobra/Adobe Stock; 6, Mark Garlick/Science Photo Library/Getty Images; 7, MR1805/iStockPhoto; 8, Vector Tradition/Adobe Stock; 9, © National Geographic Partners; 9 (bow tie), LHF Graphics/Shutterstock; 10 (LE), warpaintcobra/Adobe Stock; 10 (CTR), © National Geographic Partners; 10 (RT), Michael Rosskothen/Adobe Stock; 11, © National Geographic Partners; 12, Vector Tradition/Adobe Stock; 13, Catmando/Adobe Stock; 14 (UP), Tribalium88/Shutterstock; 14 (LO), warpaintcobra/Adobe Stock; 15, © National Geographic Partners; 16 (LE), Daniel/Adobe Stock; 16 (RT), photosvac/Adobe Stock; 17, Daniel/Adobe Stock; 18, IrynMerry/Shutterstock; 19, Daniel/Adobe Stock; 21, © Franco Tempesta; 23, © National Geographic Partners; 24, Dariush M/Shutterstock; 25 (UP LE), © National Geographic Partners; 25 (CTR RT), Michael Rosskothen/Adobe Stock; 25 (LO LE), Daniel/Adobe Stock; 27, anibal/Adobe Stock; 28 (UP), CNuisin/Adobe Stock; 28 (LO), Robert Clark/National Geographic Image Collection; 29 (UP), Design Pics Inc/National Geographic Image Collection; 29 (LO LE), Feature China/Barcroft Media via Getty Images; 29 (LO RT), Millard H. Sharp/Science Source; 30 (LE), Tom Walker/Getty Images; 30 (CTR), Roxana Bashyrova/Shutterstock; 30 (RT), USO/Getty Images; 31, © National Geographic Partners; 32, DM7/Shutterstock

Hardcover ISBN: 978-1-4263-3904-2
Reinforced library binding ISBN: 978-1-4263-3905-9

Printed in China
21/PPS/1

Where does the *T. rex* sit? Anywhere I WANT.

Tyrannosaurus rex